ANGST

—·—

Building Resilience And Self-Esteem For Girls

Dr. Barbara Becker Holstein

Enchanted Self Press

ISBN: 978-1-7367862-4-6

Copyright © 2022 by Dr. Barbara Becker Holstein

Enchanted Self Press
Long Branch NJ
USA

All rights reserved.

No portion of this book may be reproduced in any form without written permission from the publisher or author, except as permitted by U.S. copyright law.

This book is dedicated to all the young girls everywhere who may have felt unsure about themselves. They are our priceless future.

INTRODUCTION

This book is dedicated to all the young girls everywhere who may have wondered if they were weird or felt the angst and confusion of growing up. Of course in reality they are our priceless future, just needing to better understand themselves. Helping them realize their potential, talents and unique voices is what this series is all about.

As a positive psychologist I am aware of the anxiety and even depressiveness that girls can experience in the tumult of growing up. Capturing some of the actual situations that get them down and then explaining how to get past these issues is what this series is set up to do.

This book is designed to teach what normal looks and feels like and how we can get there. Each girl is offered a creative opportunity to develop her creative talents and potential as she processes and better understands the angst of growing up and how it can be successfully handled. She can bring her own talents to her thoughts and responses to the issues presented which will further take her along a road of enhanced resilience and better self esteem. She can write her creative thoughts, create poetry, start a play, draw a picture, or she can get out her phone and use it as a diary, or a means of sharing ideas about growing up with a friend, or her mom or grandma. Or she can actually make selfie films with her phone which can be a great enhancer for self esteem and sharing one's creative talents. Who knows, maybe she will be the next female famous for great filmmaking that started with her responses to Ansgt!

This book is the first in a series of books to help girls come of age with less Angst and more use of their creative talents, resilience and self esteem. The films that one has a link to at the end of each book are based on diary style fiction books that I have written for girls. These books led to selfie films that I have produced. The actresses in these films use their cell phones to do all of their scenes, on her own. My selfie films have been selected or won awards over 125 times at Film Festivals.

This book is based on the film *Angst*, featuring Megan Brown, which can be found at https://bit.ly/3YOym7n.

The world is never still. Coming of age issues will always be around, but the ways of solving them and strengthening the next generation of women will change over time. When I was little, I kept a diary and I wrote poetry. I never dreamed of myself becoming a filmmaker, author and a psychologist. I never dreamed I could carry filmmaking equipment in my pocket.

Who knows what your daughter or granddaughter will be able to do or carry in her pocket? Let's just help her to have enough resilience and self esteem to have her dreams come true.

Contents

1. I don't like the way I look in the mirror   1
2. I need my mom   5
3. I hate the new baby   9
4. I feel empty some days and I'm completely fine others   13
5. I hate my family   17
6. I feel like I'm in some sort of dream   21
7. I'm afraid that no one in my new school will like me   25
8. Save me from this loneliness   29
9. I have friends now   33
10. I'm in love   37
11. It's so confusing to love two people at the same time   41
12. I feel so miserable and so alone   45
13. I need a miracle   49
14. Some things hurt so much   53
15. Am I weird?   57

16.	Let's Talk About YOU!	61
17.	Things that make me happy	63
18.	Things that make me angry	67
19.	Things that make me sad	71
20.	Things that make me laugh	75
21.	Things that make me feel afraid	79
22.	Things I like to do	83
23.	Things I don't like to do	87
24.	If you could change the world	91
About Dr. Barbara Becker Holstein		95
Also By Dr. Holstein		97

1

I DON'T LIKE THE WAY I LOOK IN THE MIRROR

At one time or another almost all girls don't like the way they look. This can happen because of a sudden growth spurt, weight gain or loss or unfortunately someone may have made a remark that hurt. Sometimes we simply haven't become used to our new bodies as we mature. There are many ways to help ourselves be more comfortable with the way we look. Some are as simple as a new haircut. Other ways are more complex where new clothes or the style of dressing may have to change. Sometimes sharing with a parent or even a counselor may be in order, as we may be putting too much focus on our bodies. The media and the Internet sometimes makes us put too much emphasis on how we look rather than how we can develop our brains, bodies and our hearts to make the world a better place.

IMPORTANT: If you are hiding an eating disorder I encourage you not to. Go to someone you love or respect and share what is going on. The dangers can be serious, even life threatening, to let an eating disorder go.

DR. BARBARA BECKER HOLSTEIN

Write a poem, create a list or ask a question

Public   *Private*

ANGST

Write a play or say what you really think:

Public   Private

Public   Private

DR. BARBARA BECKER HOLSTEIN

Draw a picture, take a selfie, or make your own selfie film

Public																										Private

2

I NEED MY MOM

Needing our mom, dad, and often our grandparents is totally normal and really important. There is no way we can come into this world knowing how to care for ourselves or what is important for survival, pleasure, or just growing up in a safe way. We also need our parents and grandparents to not only teach us how to handle every stage of life until we are adults, but also to give love and attention to us. So when a person feels cheated, such as when a new baby may come home with mom, it really is a terrible feeling of loss. The good thing is that many parents try to make sure they still give the love needed to all their children. However moving, or a parent being sick, or a parent losing a job, can strain the household and you may be left feeling hurt and not treated fairly. I suggest honesty with parents when they slip in their job of parenting. Simply getting one's feelings out can make a big difference. No one is a mind reader. Oftentimes an easy solution like having a meal out together can make all the difference - time alone for catching up and sharing.

DR. BARBARA BECKER HOLSTEIN

Write a poem, create a list or ask a question:

Public   Private

ANGST

Write a play or say what you really think:

Public   *Private*

DR. BARBARA BECKER HOLSTEIN

Draw a picture, take a selfie, or make your own selfie film

Public   Private

3

I HATE THE NEW BABY

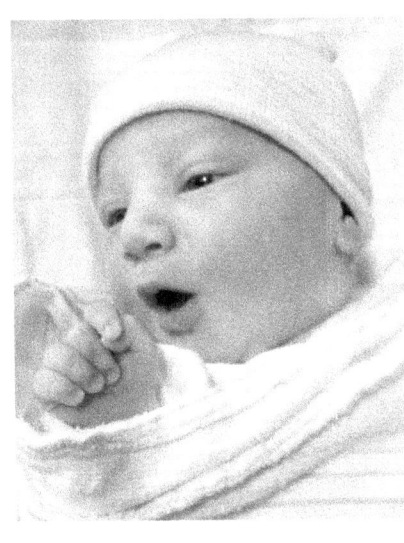

Being jealous of a new baby is a very common reaction. Suddenly a tiny infant takes up so much time and the baby just sleeps and cries. Adapting to a baby includes three steps:

1. Make sure your parents know what your needs are. For example, not to be awakened during the night.

2. Look for ways to help out. Everyone is under strain and will appreciate you pitching in when you can.

3. Observe and watch and soon you will begin to see things about the baby that may tug at your heart. My hunch is one day you will realize you like your sibling, maybe even love her.

DR. BARBARA BECKER HOLSTEIN

Write a poem, create a list or ask a question:

Public   Private

ANGST

Write a play or say what you really think:

Public   *Private*

DR. BARBARA BECKER HOLSTEIN

Draw a picture, take a selfie, or make your own selfie film

Public   Private

4

I FEEL EMPTY SOME DAYS AND I'M COMPLETELY FINE OTHERS

Feeling empty some days and great other days is a function of being alive. It's important to realize that with everything you may be asked to do in school, after school, chores at home, sports, it is natural that some days suck. Understanding what can help you on those days is important. Sometimes being honest with a parent or someone you trust can really help. Simply someone you care about giving you a hug can make the day a whole lot better. For example, one family created what they call a Family Hug. If anyone needs special cuddling or feeling loved that day, they call out Family Hug and everyone who is home comes running to create that circle of love. Simpler things can be calling a friend and getting out of your normal routine. Maybe some shopping or sitting in a park together. If feeling empty doesn't seem to go away, then you need to tell your parents or someone you trust. Some issues should be handled by people who have been trained to know how to help and lift spirits.

DR. BARBARA BECKER HOLSTEIN

Write a poem, create a list or ask a question:

Public   Private

ANGST

Write a play or say what you really think:

Public   *Private*

DR. BARBARA BECKER HOLSTEIN

Draw a picture, take a selfie, or make your own selfie film

Public   *Private*

5

I HATE MY FAMILY

Family can be very annoying. Sometimes we hate someone in our family. This is normal because it is human nature to get aggravated with people we are with a lot. Loving others does not mean they don't annoy us. Even happily married couples get annoyed at each other. We all have some habits that don't take others into account. So what to do when you hate your family?

First, figure out what it is you are hating. Is there something going on in the house that shouldn't? If that is the case, then speaking up to the right person, a safe person, such as one of your teachers or a counselor, is a good place to start. But let's assume, as usually is the case, that someone is a pest, or not being considerate to you or taking your feelings into account.

For example, your parents have started looking for a new house and not told you. You find out and 'hate' your parents for not taking your feelings into account. You would hate to have to move. Don't they care? Best way to get your answers is to talk to them. Maybe they wanted to surprise the family Talking it out can be very helpful. Having a weekly session where family can share complaints, but also solutions can be suggested and decided upon. Soon you will realize you don't hate your family anymore.

DR. BARBARA BECKER HOLSTEIN

Write a poem, create a list or ask a question:

Public   Private

ANGST

Write a play or say what you really think:

Public   *Private*

DR. BARBARA BECKER HOLSTEIN

Draw a picture, take a selfie, or make your own selfie film

Public   Private

6

I FEEL LIKE I'M IN SOME SORT OF DREAM

There are moments in everyone's life where we can feel like we are in a dream. Sometimes this happens when extremely good things happen. If you have wanted a dog for a long time and one morning your parents say "We have something for you" and you see an adorable puppy in a box, you might feel like you are in a dream. Also we can feel like we are in a dream with sudden bad news. I remember being shocked when my mom told me my grandfather had passed. She told me to pack so we could go to Boston to be with my grandmother. I was just staring at the closet feeling in a dream.

The good thing about this mental state is that it usually passes very quickly. the mind readjusts. Just give it a bit of time. For me, within 30 minutes I was busy packing. Shock, just like laughing hysterically about something or having a good cry, is just another way we have to adjust to the variety of circumstances that happen to all of us.

DR. BARBARA BECKER HOLSTEIN

Write a poem, create a list or ask a question:

Public   Private

ANGST

Write a play or say what you really think:

Public   Private

DR. BARBARA BECKER HOLSTEIN

Draw a picture, take a selfie, or make your own selfie film

Public   Private

7

I'M AFRAID THAT NO ONE IN MY NEW SCHOOL WILL LIKE ME

Being afraid is a normal human reaction to anything that arouses our anxiety. We can be afraid of a dog coming toward us not on a leash or afraid that moving to a new neighborhood will mean we have no friends. So how do we realistically handle the times in life we are afraid about - happenings that affect our relationships. The first step is feedback, to judge how the situation is likely to play out.

As far as moving and making friends, ask your parents and grandparents how they made friends when they moved. Then think about their suggestions. For example, your mom may have made friends by being friendly, your dad may have developed friends as he played on a sports team. Grandma may remember her mom making cookies for the neighborhood kids of all ages and that did it.

Soon you will see that making friends usually means being kind, interested in others and not getting too uptight. As far as a dog not on a leash, walk in the other direction!

DR. BARBARA BECKER HOLSTEIN

Write a poem, create a list or ask a question:

Public   Private

ANGST

Write a play or say what you really think:

Public   *Private*

DR. BARBARA BECKER HOLSTEIN

Draw a picture, take a selfie, or make your own selfie film

Public   *Private*

8

SAVE ME FROM THIS LONELINESS

We are all lonely sometimes. Sometimes we are lonely just because a friend is out of town. Perhaps she is at camp for a month and you are stuck at home. Sometimes we are lonely for more complex reasons like a grandparent is sick and can't visit anymore. It's unpleasant at best, so how do we handle loneliness successfully?

First figure out why you are lonely. Is there anything you can do to fix it? Call a different friend? Call your grandma on the phone and cheer her up? Go to the library and get a good book? Make a new friend? Pray? Tell your mom or dad. cry. pull yourself together? The truth is loneliness is so unique that I can't give you a clear answer. Sometimes we just pray for a miracle. Nothing is wrong if it works for you. The good news is that loneliness passes. It is an emotion and emotions are not permanent. Usually action is the best way to give loneliness a little push to get on its way. What has worked for you?

DR. BARBARA BECKER HOLSTEIN

Write a poem, create a list or ask a question:

Public   Private

ANGST

Write a play or say what you really think:

Public   Private

DR. BARBARA BECKER HOLSTEIN

Draw a picture, take a selfie, or make your own selfie film

Public   Private

9

I HAVE FRIENDS NOW

Having friends after not having friends for a while is a delight, but can still be filled with some concerns. Now one has to keep them. The simplest way to keep friends is to be yourself, often your best self. Some suggestions: 1. Be a good listener. 2. Don't gossip about a friend to other kids. 3. Don't tease friends.4. Don't bully. 5.Be kind and generous.

Perhaps you are the one that plans a surprise birthday party for a friend.

Perhaps you are the one that helps a friend memorize her part in a school play.

Perhaps you can....................I'm sure you can come up with wonderful ways to keep and even add more friends

DR. BARBARA BECKER HOLSTEIN

Write a poem, create a list or ask a question:

Public   *Private*

ANGST

Write a play or say what you really think:

Public   *Private*

DR. BARBARA BECKER HOLSTEIN

Draw a picture, take a selfie, or make your own selfie film

Public   Private

10

I'M IN LOVE

Part of growing up is having crushes on others or even feeling we have fallen in love with someone. These feelings are part of life, usually growing stronger as we leave childhood and become young teens. I had my first crush when I was 10. The only person I ever told was Angela, my bestie friend. I don't think Paul ever knew I had a crush on him.

My second crush years later was on Bob and again it was Jill, a best friend in junior high that I told. The angst of these crushes and feeling in love can be exhausting. Mothers and grandmothers can be very helpful if you let them into your private world of ecstasy and agony. Good luck and I can almost guarantee that someday you will be laughing and telling your children some of the highs and lows of a crush or feeling in love.

DR. BARBARA BECKER HOLSTEIN

Write a poem, create a list or ask a question:

Public					Private

ANGST

Write a play or say what you really think:

Public   *Private*

DR. BARBARA BECKER HOLSTEIN

Draw a picture, take a selfie, or make your own selfie film

Public   Private

11

IT'S SO CONFUSING TO LOVE TWO PEOPLE AT THE SAME TIME

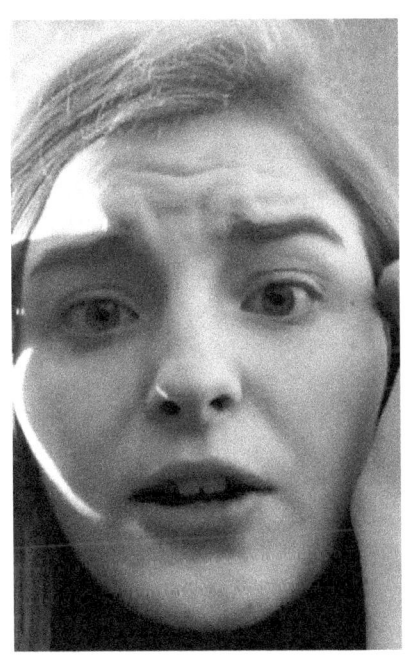

Growing up moves fast. We move from playing with dolls to makeup and dating in a few years. It is amazing to suddenly have crushes, have a period, date or hang around with both sexes, perhaps being lured into potentially dangerous situations such as drugs or early sex. The mind can hardly keep up with all the challenges of growing up. What keeps you safe and sure about life and your own capacities to make decisions?

It is your resilient nature combined with: self-esteem, awareness of your potential, your talents, your limitations, and having people in your life you can go to. My hunch is you have all the above. Go ahead, welcome the future as it arrives. Yes, your dreams can come true and some day you will look in the mirror and welcome a talented, resilient woman as your bestie forever.

DR. BARBARA BECKER HOLSTEIN

Write a poem, create a list or ask a question:

Public   Private

ANGST

Write a play or say what you really think:

Public   *Private*

DR. BARBARA BECKER HOLSTEIN

Draw a picture, take a selfie, or make your own selfie film

Public											Private

12

I FEEL SO MISERABLE AND SO ALONE

Most of us have felt miserable at one time or another. Misery can happen for many reasons: not being understood, feeling left out, being disappointed, being jealous of a sibling. Also for things that happen, like having to move, or failing a test, or a friend dropping us.

Misery is a temporary state of being that we want to move out. Some ways to move away from misery are to exercise, call a friend, share your pain, do something that you really enjoy doing, or sometimes just a good night's rest. Sometimes the best thing to do is to confront the situation and talk to the right person or ask your parents for help in dealing with the issue that led to misery.

DR. BARBARA BECKER HOLSTEIN

Write a poem, create a list or ask a question:

Public					Private

ANGST

Write a play or say what you really think:

Public   Private

DR. BARBARA BECKER HOLSTEIN

Draw a picture, take a selfie, or make your own selfie film

Public   Private

13

I NEED A MIRACLE

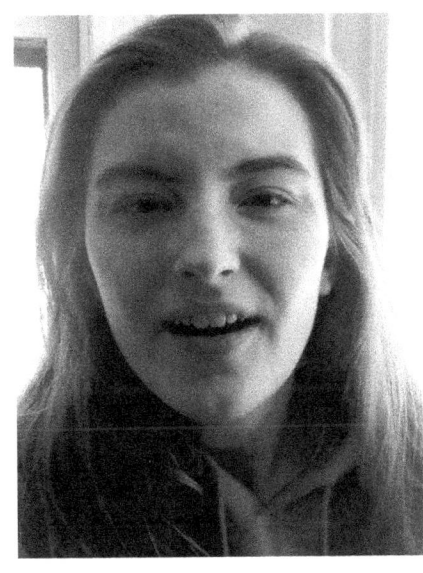

Most of us at one time or another wish a miracle would happen. We find ourselves in the middle of a situation that is difficult or hurtful or worrisome and we simply can't seem to find a way out. Calling on a miracle is normal and it can reduce the stress of the moment. However it may be even more helpful to go over the problem with someone you trust, and see if there is a way to move toward a solution. For example, when I was 12 we moved and the new school seemed to have placed mc randomly in certain classes that were too easy for me. I felt miserable as I had worked so hard in 6th grade and like the pace of somewhat challenging classes. I spoke to my father and he suggested I talk to my guidance counselor. I did and she changed my classes! I was thrilled and didn't need a miracle after all, or you could say a miracle happened. Life was good again.

DR. BARBARA BECKER HOLSTEIN

Write a poem, create a list or ask a question:

Public   Private

ANGST

Write a play or say what you really think:

Public   Private

DR. BARBARA BECKER HOLSTEIN

Draw a picture, take a selfie, or make your own selfie film

Public   *Private*

14

SOME THINGS HURT SO MUCH

The truth is, in life, some things do hurt much more than others. Parents divorcing may hurt much more than a friend moving. The death of a grandparent may leave a much bigger hole in your heart than your pet rabbit dying. The difference is the toll a loss takes on you and how resilient you are as you grow up to handle different problems and losses. Here are some ideas to cope with hurt: 1. Allow yourself to cry, tears can cleanse and help you feel better. 2. Share your pain with any and all of the right people: parents, friends, grandparents, teachers or other safe people in your life. 3. Indulge yourself in treats and time to heal. 4. Work with a counselor or therapist to come to grips with something that hurts if it just won't go away, or to find a solution to the problem.

DR. BARBARA BECKER HOLSTEIN

Write a poem, create a list or ask a question:

Public *Private*

ANGST

Write a play or say what you really think:

Public *Private*

DR. BARBARA BECKER HOLSTEIN

Draw a picture, take a selfie, or make your own selfie film

Public   Private

15

AM I WEIRD?

As we grow up we have so many different feelings, thoughts, ideas, and moods. This is all normal, yet at times we can feel like we are weird, different from others, maybe strange. I was very fortunate growing up that my mother and father encouraged me to be myself. That is the most important message that one can receive about oneself. Coming to admire, accept and thrive with yourself is the way to keep becoming an amazing person who has values, ideas, plans, resilience, talents and, in the long term, lots of potential. Remember it is great to love yourself. After all, as someone said, everyone else is taken!

DR. BARBARA BECKER HOLSTEIN

Write a poem, create a list or ask a question:

Public   Private

ANGST

Write a play or say what you really think:

Public   *Private*

DR. BARBARA BECKER HOLSTEIN

Draw a picture, take a selfie, or make your own selfie film

Public										Private

16

Let's Talk About YOU!

You can see all of these situations acted out in the *Angst* film, located at https://bit.ly/3YOymZn

Before you view the film however, let's talk more about you.

17

THINGS THAT MAKE ME HAPPY

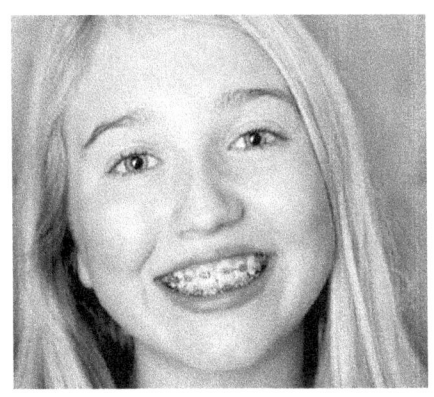

Feeling happy is one of those unique emotions that most of us yearn for. We often remember each detail of an event or moment or celebration when we felt happy. It is hard to explain what it feels like to be happy, but we all know when we are happy.

There have been songs written about being happy, poems about happiness. movies devoted to endings where everyone is happy and books that often end with the main characters happy. I hope that you can take this opportunity to remember some of the times when you have been happy and share them below. Perhaps you will keep those times private, but if you care to share them with your parents or friends, it will be fun, perhaps perplexing and interesting to see that what makes one person happy would never be what makes someone else happy.

DR. BARBARA BECKER HOLSTEIN

Write a poem, create a list or ask a question:

Public   Private

ANGST

Write a play or say what you really think:

Public

Private

DR. BARBARA BECKER HOLSTEIN

Draw a picture, take a selfie, or make your own selfie film

Public   *Private*

18

THINGS THAT MAKE ME ANGRY

Everyone gets angry at least once and awhile. Like being happy or sad, anger is another human emotion. In everyday life anger sweeps over someone for a while and then the person calms down. As she calms down the feelings of anger quiet or disappear and often at that point she finds a way to move forward without anger.

The ways to help get rid of anger can include exercise, distractions, keeping a journal, getting a good night's sleep and efforts to solve a problem that may be accounting for the anger.

Here is your chance to look at anger in your life. Please share any solutions you figure out about handling anger.

DR. BARBARA BECKER HOLSTEIN

Write a poem, create a list or ask a question:

ANGST

Write a play or say what you really think:

Public   Private

69

DR. BARBARA BECKER HOLSTEIN

Draw a picture, take a selfie, or make your own selfie film

Public   *Private*

19

THINGS THAT MAKE ME SAD

Feeling sad is for most people not pleasant. Usually feeling sad means something bad has happened or we are disappointed in the outcome of an event. Big or small things in life can make us feel sad for a while. The reasons vary from person to person. One person may be sad for a while when summer is over as she loves the beach, while a friend may be glad as she hates the heat.

What makes you sad? Is there anything you can do about it? Perhaps talking to your parents about what makes you sad can lead to some changes and positive solutions.

When I was young I was very sad because I wanted to take piano lessons. When I clearly shared with my parents that time was passing and I really needed to start lessons, they had found a teacher for me within a week.

DR. BARBARA BECKER HOLSTEIN

Write a poem, create a list or ask a question:

Public   Private

ANGST

Write a play or say what you really think:

Public   *Private*

DR. BARBARA BECKER HOLSTEIN

Draw a picture, take a selfie, or make your own selfie film

Public   Private

20

THINGS THAT MAKE ME LAUGH

One of the best things in life that doesn't cost a penny or require any study is a good laugh.

A deep belly laugh can make us feel uplifted, happy, full of energy and keep a smile on our face for hours. I like to think of a good laugh as a way to give a massage to my insides. Some people love to watch dogs playing the piano on youtube or cats unrolling toilet paper. Some laugh just by getting together with friends, having popcorn, and sharing the news of the day knowing that something said will lead to a lot of laughter.

What makes you laugh?

DR. BARBARA BECKER HOLSTEIN

Write a poem, create a list or ask a question:

Public   Private

ANGST

Write a play or say what you really think:

Public   Private

DR. BARBARA BECKER HOLSTEIN

Draw a picture, take a selfie, or make your own selfie film

Public   Private

21

THINGS THAT MAKE ME FEEL AFRAID

When we are very small it is not uncommon to be afraid of the dark or thinking something scary is under the bed. Our parents, grandparents, daycare teachers or babysitters teach us about life. But sometimes when we are older we are afraid of certain things and feel uneasy or even shy to tell others. It is helpful to know that we all have things we are afraid of: a bully in the school yard or making new friends.

Lots of times parents can really help get rid of our fears. When I moved once my mom said she would make a pizza party for some of the girls I met and liked. I was afraid but with her encouragement the party took place and I had great new friends.

What are some things you might be afraid of? Can you think of any solutions to your fears?

DR. BARBARA BECKER HOLSTEIN

Write a poem, create a list or ask a question:

Public							Private

ANGST

Write a play or say what you really think:

Public   Private

DR. BARBARA BECKER HOLSTEIN

Draw a picture, take a selfie, or make your own selfie film

Public   Private

22

THINGS I LIKE TO DO

There is almost nothing better than really liking to do something and getting to do it. When we can do what most suits us, it brings all the best parts of ourselves together. For instance, if you want to take tap dancing and you get to do it and you are good at it, it can feel like you are not only amazing, but you feel filled with joy and anticipation, when you are in class or even dancing on the porch at home in your tap shoes. However if your parents suggested that you play the drums you might immediately feel in your gut that you would hate doing that. Hopefully your parents would not make you.

From what kind of frosting on a cakc we like, to what we want to do when we grow up, everyone has different answers. I'm interesed in knowing what you find you like a lot, whether it is ginger cookies or learning, hanging out with friends or reading about ancient Egypt.

DR. BARBARA BECKER HOLSTEIN

Write a poem, create a list or ask a question:

Public   Private

ANGST

Write a play or say what you really think:

Public   Private

DR. BARBARA BECKER HOLSTEIN

Draw a picture, take a selfie, or make your own selfie film

Public   Private

23

THINGS I DON'T LIKE TO DO

As great as it is to like to do certain things, like is not always about the things we like to do. There are also things we don't like to do, but must at times. You may hate to go to the dentist, but your parents still make you go twice a year or more if there are problems. You maybe hate to clean your room, yet have to do it. Of course, if you feel made to do something that is inappropriate, you should tell someone you trust.

I hated to clean my room. Hanging up clothes was the worst. One day I found my room locked and a note on it saying I couldn't sleep in there until I cleaned it. I was angry but I didn't like sleeping in a dark and almost empty guest bedroom. So I cleaned my room. Did I dislike doing it? Yes.

What do you dislike?

DR. BARBARA BECKER HOLSTEIN

Write a poem, create a list or ask a question:

Public   *Private*

ANGST

Write a play or say what you really think:

Public   Private

Draw a picture, take a selfie, or make your own selfie film

Public   Private

24

IF YOU COULD CHANGE THE WORLD

If you could change the world in any way you wanted, what would you change? And if you have ideas on how to change what you see as wrong, please list those ideas also.

I hope you will put on your thinking cap and really give some thought to how you would change the world. YOU are our future, whether you think of yourself that way or not. With opportunities for education, mentors, time to grow up and time to thrive you can become one of the heroines of our time. You may invent something that only you could do, or help people with special training that you get that saves lives, or discover something that leads to better medicine or ways of living.

I can't wait to read what you want to change and how it could be changed. You can reach me at barbara.holstein@gmail.com

DR. BARBARA BECKER HOLSTEIN

Write a poem, create a list or ask a question:

Public   Private

ANGST

Write a play or say what you really think:

Public   Private

DR. BARBARA BECKER HOLSTEIN

Draw a picture, take a selfie, or make your own selfie film

Public   Private

ABOUT DR. BARBARA BECKER HOLSTEIN

Dr. Barbara Becker Holstein, internationally known Positive Psychologist is the creator of The Enchanted Self®, a positive psychology method for happiness and a pioneer in Selfies as Film. Dr. Holstein's Enchanted Self website, EnchantedSelf.com, was included as one of the best websites in positive psychology. She is in private practice in Long Branch, New Jersey with her husband, Dr. Russell M. Holstein.

Dr. Barbara can be found on the web, interviewed, writing articles and posting video 'TED' style talks on happiness, Positive Psychology, relationships and parenting. Her Roku channel is: The Enchanted Self Presents.

She has been a contributor to Your Tango, Heart and Soul, The Philadelphia Inquirer, Honey Good, Cosmopolitan Magazine, Redbook, Real Simple, Women's World, The Wall Street Journal, Psychcentral.com, Time online, the Today Show and Family Circle Magazine.

ALSO BY DR. HOLSTEIN

This book is based on the film, *Angst*. To watch the film, go to https://bit.ly/3YOymZn.

Books

THE TRUTH SERIES FOR GIRLS

The Truth: Diary of a Gutsy Tween

Secrets: Diary of a Gutsy Teen

Conflict and a Bit of Magic

OTHER BOOKS

The Truth: I'm A Girl, I'm Smart and I Know Everything

Secrets: You Tell Me Yours, I'll Tell You Mine - Maybe

Recipes for Enchantment, The Secret Ingredient is YOU!

THE ENCHANTED SELF, a Positive Therapy

Seven Gateways to Happiness: Freeing Your Enchanted Self

Delight, There Comes a Time in Every Woman's Life for Delight!

A Selfie Film: Falling In Love

7 Ways to Help Your Family Recover From the Pandemic

Next Year In Jerusalem: Around Every Corner, Mystery and Romance

Next Year In Jerusalem: Romance, Mystery and Spiritual Awakenings

FILMS:

Lock Down:

Lock Down Trailer

The Truth A Short Film:

Secrets A Coming Of Age Selfie Film:

Falling In Love A Coming Of Age Selfie Film:

Truth is Stranger Than Fiction:

Life Is Complicated:

Truths Change And Still Remain:

Conflict:

Angst:

Selfie:

The Medium, A Coming of Age, Selfie Film:

ANGST

The Selfie Project Pilot:

Conflict and a Bit of Magic, A Coming of Age, Selfie Film:

I Had An Affair - Or Did I?:

I Had An Affair With My Husband:

Around Every Corner - Part 1:

Delight

Do Dreams Come True?

www.ingramcontent.com/pod-product-compliance
Lightning Source LLC
Chambersburg PA
CBHW072213070526
44585CB00015B/1320